The Natural Order of Things

poems by

Richard Donze

Finishing Line Press
Georgetown, Kentucky

The Natural Order of Things

Publisher: Leah Huete de Maines
Editor: Christen Kincaid
Cover Art: Photo and Painting in photo by Kathleen Donze
Author Photo: MK Photo
Cover Design: Elizabeth Maines McCleavy

Order online: www.finishinglinepress.com
            also available on amazon.com

Author inquiries and mail orders:
Finishing Line Press
P. O. Box 1626
Georgetown, Kentucky 40324
U. S. A.

Table of Contents

For Kathy, who stepped into my kitchen and my world as I was working on that Yeats "Byzantium" paper, only the first of many signs that there would always be poetry in our lives.

I

Springhouse

I am trying to imagine 1760
when the website says they
built this one and looking at
it now in winter under bare
beech branches with cluster

of white pines on the hill a
hundred yards away also
imagining the likely chance
discovery improved by trial
and error over maybe years
decades maybe centuries that
a house about 10 feet square

over creek trickle angled
just so into sloping ground
with just so much below
grade and above under a
wood shingled moss magnet
roof with walls whose blue
stones look perfectly sized

and spaced with mortar to
cover their likely multitude
of misshapen sins when the
ground gave them up to 18th
century low tech shovel and
pick ax would keep any eggs
milk and meat stored inside

from spoiling in summer or
freezing in winter not the
first and certainly not the
last proud bulwark against
the natural order of things.

local strawberries

come late
May early
June to

the north
east smaller
sweeter deeper

red more
tender than
anything sooner

or later
from south
or west

short life
pick ripe
eat now

II

we are expecting

some snow
this winter

we are expecting

a baby
in May

we are expecting

snow maybe
May baby

Nesting

I already had a hand on the
doorknob when she asked
if I'd mind
if we didn't

she half apologized for
not being herself for
not being more light-hearted she
said the hormones were changing
her you could see that
she said she felt

less like
going out for libation and
more like
staying home for vitamins

less like
arranging the social calendar and
more like
re-arranging the furniture

with the belly bulge came
two kinds of weight
two kinds of heavy
the first made her back hurt
the second a seriousness a
responsibility a
need to provide
here's how for my
somehow the

woman the
stronger
must provide this she said

normalcy would return
after it was over knowing
of course it never would

smiling at her beautiful lie I
took off jacket
emptied pockets of
wallet keys change for
the meter changed
on-the-town shoes for
around-the-house slippers and
asked where she wanted
that balloon picture hung

Diapers and course

there were the obligate new tasks
 how to fold a blanket just so
 upside down delta
 apex over feet and legs
 left angle tucked under her left side
 right under her right a swaddled
 streamlined package you could
 carry on your forearm and would
 stay that way when you put it down
 just so

and lots of weight to lose
 280 days of inches and pounds
 and much more than that of self
 becoming other

lighter and liking it
 so many things we used to do
 and liked to do
 now shouldn't do
 and couldn't do
 and quite frankly
 don't care to do
 simpler

getting down to lean
 over her unwrapped tiny bottom
 inspecting exploring the folds
 nooks and crannies for the
 flecks and specks that escaped
 a broad washcloth wipe sweep
 before re-wrapping
 just so

sensing all the
just-right temperatures

going on
just-too-little sleep

changing crib sheets and schedules
diapers and course

Rained through the night

I got out of bed to see
if and where water was coming in
not selectively specifically scientifically
not estimating wind direction or velocity
just shuffling room to room
feeling screens sweeping
hands across sills closing
windows where wet eyes
half closed not to lose
the sleeping groove

stopping last in Liza's room
wondering if thunder had
summoned her attention from
wherever it was
wondering if loudness and darkness and
suddenness could make something
unfamiliar frightening wondering
if she had learned yet to
fear something unfamiliar instead of
trying to eat it

her door creaked opening
her squeezy bunny squeaked underfoot
her window rattled closing as a
gush of cool spray pelted my lower
abdomen and thighs

she was lying curled in the
crib corner against the bumpers
covers kicked off
socks pulled off
teddy thrown clear of the sleeping zone
fingers intertwined with blanket edges weaving
a new fabric

she had slept through it all
including my clumsiness
either more tired than curious or
something in her dreams more
compelling than thunder and rain

Little Liza asked

When leaves die do
they go to heaven?

the yellow maple
and brick-red oak
she liked so much
on the tree or soft
as hundreds of tiny
pillows in the jump-
ing pile smooth and
cool the tulip poplar
cat mask against her
cheeks and supple
the three lobes of
golden sassafras her
fingers could bend
and move like heads
and arms now brown-
ing brittling curling
stiff we might discuss

bacteria ingesting di-
gesting them back to
soil nitrogen cycles
she couldn't see or
get just yet but look-

ing up we could both
see the November twi-
light the forecasted
variable clouds the sun
finishing here and on
its way to California
and across the Pacific
carrying tomorrow but

not before one last bit
of business after drop-
ping fast behind bran-
ches that every day
hide less of orange
ball slipping below
darkening dusky gray
horizon line to explode
back up sky on fire
blazing orange

The leaves don't, I told
her, but their colors do

arithmetic

adding
a child
wondering
what we'll
get by
subtracting
time from
sleep and
personal
indulgence both
already near
zero

worrying
that
dividing
love between
two benefits
neither

remembering
that
whenever
Jesus talked
about love
and heaven
and other
wonderful things
He always
multiplied.

April 23rd

was unusually cold
record cold
the rain changed
to snow and
back and forth
all day white
dusting daffodil and
dogwood amazing
Elizabeth whose
books always
pictured winter
and spring
on separate pages
and surprising me

before stopping that
night when a
lambent blur behind
wind-shifted clouds
gathered to full moon

Kathy's ninth hard moon
of nine very
hard moons of
weighting and waiting
to finally sit up
holding knees and breath and
push push push
that's it keep pushing
out little Sarah Hope
who found our voices
familiar but the
air dry and
unusually cold

record cold
the rain changed
to snow and
back and forth
all day surprising
Elizabeth and
amazing me.

Sally Hope asked

where do the
lightning bugs go

(now you see them by the closing day lilies)

every summer dawn with
first light to hide them little
star pieces fall from the sky

(now you don't and the crickets won't say where)

wait all day in the grass for
that space between no longer
day and not yet night to rise

(now you see them down the hill by the drooping wild grape)

blinking on to see their
way and off to save their
light then picking a spot

(now you don't erased into the dark)

between Jupiter and Polaris
hold their backs together and
blink on ready for your wish

(now you see them)

Jesus and Jewelweed

Sally and Liza like
jewelweed like it
twice first looking
and smelling the
red-spotted orange
trumpet flower that
spreads so easily
along late summer
back road shoulder
waste ground and
creek banks second

looking for the
plump green pods
that spring open
at the lightest
touch to scatter
seeds and like

its second name
what Jesus said
to Magdalen after
his fat tomb
had sprung open
at an angel's
lightest touch

touch me not

who might have
also liked jewelweed
and talked about
the kingdom of
heaven being like

late summer back
road shoulders and
waste ground creek
banks where touching
and not touching
scatters good seed

We look to the sky

driving home from
Christmas dinner
we look to the sky
clearly through the winter

windshield wiper wiped
zone orange swirl and
indigo stripe behind
December see-through

trees in the back seat
little Liza blinks at
telephone poles ticking
past us the other way

half dreaming re-playing
the afternoon thinking
about Jesus whose birthday
it was today thinking about

Pinocchio whose story she
heard today in Uncle
George's lap the book he
gave her we look to the sky

first star Venus maybe
not she says maybe
Gepetto's wishing star
maybe

maybe the star the wise
men followed to Bethlehem
maybe
then home and dark and

outside we look to the sky
all stars now there's the
Dipper and 1 2 3 in a line
Orion's belt but where's

Venus somewhere up
there waiting for us
to wish and follow
we look to the sky

Thea asked

do you still get
butterflies when you
see her after all
this time an odd
question at the work-
station counter where
they usually discussed
diagnostic scans and
treatment plans but she

was only two days away
from the day to briefly
trade her short white
clinic cloak for long
white gown and vows
and she worried about
love being long-lived
and his answer just as
odd:

something happens you
could call butterflies
a metamorphosis a
change of state from
the crawling clay-bound
caterpillar I occasionally
am back to when I flitted
and floated flower to

meadow flower collecting
nectar at the tip of an
uncoiled spiral hollow
tongue and the first
time I saw her the
sweetest best saved
for last when wind

in wild carrot was
music and I
could fly

Watering flowers

in the no-rain
July dusk as
cicadas clocked out
to cricket shift
under pinking skies

he saw her
in the kitchen
window bustling a
late-start dinner in
the strapless bathing
suit she had no time
to change just back
from the neighbor's
pool her head face

shoulders collarbones
neatly framed above
the sill he saw her
more beautiful than
the 30-plus-years-ago
first time he saw her
more beautiful than
their baby-making-
raising days more
beautiful than the
gently drinking
geranium at his

feet she left the
frame and pots and
pans in progress as
he noticed the
stream had strayed
off mark soaking
his sneaks and
puddling the mulch

lights came on
upstairs as he
turned to hose
hydrangea

III

I carry your name (a)

50 years ago before we were
so mindful of mindfulness a
12th grade English teacher told
our after-school creative writing
class that reading would make
us better writers and meditation
better readers with better focus
better able to let distractions
pass and while fragments of
what we read are mostly brain
buried and surface only rarely
like mastodon bones and tusks
exposed by permafrost thaw
or desert sand erosion and
what we wrote lost forever I
have remembered every day
ever since to follow the breath
at the tip of my nose and when
thoughts arrive (as they always
do) to label them "thinking" and
return to the breath so today

when you would have been
70 and thoughts about you
arrive unlabeled but laden
I follow your breath from the
the tip of your nose and into
your throat where a few
months shy of 68 years ago
it stopped blocked and though
cradle-bound barely 4 weeks
old I couldn't know the way I
can know now the sadness
and fear in the house on the
walls in the air following it
now trying to read it now I
see how it might have

descended on me imprinted
on me making me remember
every day ever since to be
sad and afraid it was 34

days before that night I
arrived with a first and last
but no middle name and only
13 days after that night they
dragged themselves out of
their shock and grief and
sadness and fear and brought
me to chrism cross anointing
and holy water sprinkling and
gave me your name (in the
name of the father) in the
middle of mine (and of the
son they lost) and every day
ever since I carry your name
as homage as weight your
memory alive on me in me
in ways I didn't know couldn't
know till now as I read it in
the middle of who I am full
of sadness and fear for what

happened and why and how a
common cold and cough could
have such an uncommon awful
effect on you Mom always said
croup while Dad held a throat-
closing theory allergy to the
chocolate penicillin the doctor
ordered a few hours earlier before the house call that night
he was there right there when
your breath stopped trying to
revive you but trained and
practicing before it might be

expected he could and would
and should grab any pointy
thing—pencil pen kitchen
knife—to get the air outside
your throat inside through a
pointy-thing-shaped hole
to become breath in lungs
keeping blood red that
finally turned blue as an

older child a boy a teen
even a younger man I didn't
couldn't understand the sadness after all you were just
a baby how much could anyone have connected with and
later miss a 2-year-old 2-year-
olds barely talk and don't really
do anything the way an older
child a boy a teen even a younger man might define "do" and
"anything" or the value of either
or both and then I have my
own children and know instantly
and looking at Mom and Dad I
tried to imagine but never fully
because it hurt too much to
go too deeply into that bottom-
less sadness well where they
sunk after the worst nightmare
imaginable and had to wonder
did it mean it could and would
and will happen again maybe

to the still-fragile cradle-bound
4-week-old me while the storm
whirled above and around the
me with no middle name (yet)
she has to tend to our 5

year old brother during that
awful hour when Dad rode with
you in the ambulance and came
back long-faced swollen-eyed
but after that she's too grief-
struck-sad-numb she has to
give me to Dad's brother a
while till she gets her bearings
or some semblance (but she
won't remember any of this
later even when I grow up
and learn it from the uncle
she will say it didn't happen
and even when I go to that
uncle's funeral and see the
easeled black-and-white photo
of the smiling uncle lifting a
diapered bare-chested smiling
unquestionably little me into
the air in unquestionably the
uncle's house the stairs the
living room layout I remember
from when I was older she
still said it didn't happen) and

even in her grief still Catholic
before she even had time to
realize how enraged at and
betrayed by God she feels she
finds a way only 13 days after
that Monday night to get me to
a Sunday chrism cross anointing and holy water sprinkling
and later with children of my
own and imagining the sadness I wonder how did they
even do that so soon after
that awful night and sure the
aunts and uncles helped

but maybe a different kind
of fear drove them while
still Catholic to be sure that
just in case it happened to
me too (as it most certainly
could) that baptized at least
I could get into heaven and
not be limbo-bound and
there and then they gave
me your name the one I
carry in the middle of mine
every day ever since even

beyond forgetting denying
my brief uncle stay Mom
did not like talking about it
always got a faraway look
a stare into the space the
heart hole that stayed open
never completely closing or
filling in a dark place she
really didn't want to revisit
but sometimes hints about it
slipped out as when she said
she couldn't watch I Love Lucy
reruns because it was on TV
that Monday night April 7th
9-9:30 when everything was
happening so fast the doctor
there not grabbing any pointy
thing (your certificate listed 10
PM as the death time) Season
1 Episode 26 "The Marriage
License" about the joke Ricky
played on Lucy about the misspelling on the document that
might mean they weren't really
married and wondering now
first why didn't anyone think

to turn off the TV but then of

course of course probably
no one even knew it was
on but maybe did Mom
catch some hear some ab-
sorb some plot or dialogue
as background as osmotic
drip maybe making her wonder wish a mistake on that
death certificate the cruelest
of cruel jokes a wonder wish
maybe it wasn't you not your
name a typo a misspelling or
now trying to read the sadness and fear a wonder wish
maybe a mistake on my first
birth certificate with no middle name or a mistake 13
days after you were gone
to add yours one 95+

surviving mother-brother
uncle still clearly remembers the sadness but no-
thing else no other details
nothing about the name
and older cousins alive
at the time old enough to
attend the funeral but not
old enough then to remem-
ber much or too old now to
recall much of what was
remembered only remem-
ber that terrible wave of
sadness and grief over-
spreading the wider family
except the one cousin al-
most 12 then almost 80

now can't forget seeing
that baby so little in that
tiny casket but no other
details nothing about the
name so with Mom and
Dad gone and wishing
I'd asked more I am
forced now to explore
on my own state records
church records others'
memory fragments my
own imagination and
reading and following
the breath when thoughts
arrive (as they always do)
and now asking you and

wondering what would you
have been like looked like
sounded like lost your hair
or kept it been lean or fought
weight and blood pressure
played an instrument brought
it to Christmas Eve dinner
carol singalongs sung played
tennis bowled hunted been
doctor lawyer butcher baker
banker scientist fought in
Nam fled to Canada voted
D or R finished college sales-
man tradesman stayed local
moved away married single
fathered children other nieces
and nephews I will never know
been retired by now as our
older brother is or still working
as I am still have been called
Donnie or lost the nie and
become Don or Donald Mom

and Dad always said you
looked like a combination
of me and the one that
came after me that leap
of faith or irrational illogical
senseless optimism when
I was barely 2 the age you
were when it happened to
you and what happened to
you could've happened to
me and to any baby after
me to have another baby
another boy and 6 years
after that a final baby a
fifth of five liveborn and
fourth of four still alive a
girl it could happen to too
but maybe they already
knew without being taught
when it arrived to label it
fear and return to the
breath optimism maybe

born of believing lightning
couldn't strike twice in the
same place what are the
chances when of course
it always can no matter
how long the time and
odds and of course it
usually doesn't common
things are common and
uncommon things un-
common we didn't know
then but learned later or
at least learned to imagine
as parents ourselves how
it must've been on Mom
and Dad Dad dealing with

his own grief but having to
go back to work to keep
the roof overhead the food
on the table for Mom our
older brother and me and
also hold up Mom whose
grief was unimaginably
worse her distraction so
absolute he had to insist

his brother look after me a
while and maybe because
of that early separation just
barely 4 weeks old cradle-
bound taken from numb
caregiver and protector
that lightning strike electric
fear in the air that descended imprinted on me that
night you in the ambulance
most likely already gone
then Dad coming home
confirming what Mom most
likely already feared already
knew before you left saw
on the doctor's face saw on
yours already blue became
a seed a germ waiting till I
had my own babies to sprout
into thinking since the worst
thing that could happen
did happen it can happen
again and almost certainly
will unless unless maybe

there's something I can do
to keep it from happening
a big really big maybe but
convincing me there's no

way I can stop it unless I
keep watching for it watching watching an unconscious
solemn vow to watch and not
be taken by surprise the way
Mom Dad our older brother
the aunts the uncles even the
doctor were taken by surprise

with you watching watching
always prepared always
scanning like the scout on
the ridge looking for whatever
enemy might threaten ready
to sound the alarm on the
lookout for that threat that
thought of a possible second
lightning strike always ready
to defend against it if and
when it arrived even though
not sure how and not labeling
it thinking not returning to the
breath not even breathing
holding breath always be-
lieving it is just about to
strike wherever there's a
dark cloud a wet air whiff
of approaching storm here
now any moment any sec-
ond now and when it doesn't
not thinking what was I thinking I was crazy to think that
there was never any there
there instead labeling it
dodged this time the storm
clouds broke the lightning
flashed but never struck
but next time yes next time
that could be the time and

carrying your name I also
carry all your pain that awful awful pain of losing
breath so focused on our-
selves we never thought
about never wondered till
now what it was like for
you losing breath turning
blue did you kick writhe
thrash how did it feel to
feel so helpless in your
mother's arms and even
the doctor standing there
lacking knowledge skills
or guts to open your throat
to feel so helpless in a place
that always made you safe

and the one time you needed comfort and security like
you had never needed them
before and she couldn't do
it like the mother in the painting in the church where your
tiny casket lay where I had
my chrism cross anointing
and holy water sprinkling
holding the baby who ran to
her so fast his sandal came
undone so scared by angels
carrying a cross a lance so
scared seeking her perpetual
help but she couldn't protect
him either so with your name

they also gave me the prayer
the wish the charge to make
sure no children ever suffer
like that again no parents

ever suffer like that again
and now your fears and
hers and his and theirs in
the house on the walls in
the air that descended on
the cradle-bound 4-week
old and loaded into your
name they gave me and
now that germ that seed
that sprouted that thinks
fears lightning can strike
twice and three and four
times in the same place
why not what's to stop it
the lesson the labeled
thought planted imprinted
I remember every day ever
since and wish I could forget because it turns all
common molehills into

uncommon mountains
where every cough and
cold can close a throat
and stop breath the way
it stopped yours fearing
those commonest of
common coughs but also
fevers lumps bumps rash-
es and double that triple
that quadruple that double
quadruple quintuple that
for the demics du decade
where that fear says my
charges will be the ones
needing the used-up ven-
tilators never the ones
that never get symptoms
or get mild ones and recov-

er uneventfully at home
and of course relieved

when they come through
OK and of course not re-
lieved for long there's always next time for the
common-uncommon dance
all because of the uncom-
mon impact of a common
thing on you a fear driving
me distracted first to library
textbooks and later when
the world wide web opens
wide another world to trap
me without barriers of miles
to drive or closing times
the library is now open
all day every day just a
bootup login away and
to be sure the worst thing

doesn't happen I learn to
always expect it glossing
over rejecting the simple
common things and from
there an easy path a short
walk to the uncommon thing
the worse thing and not just
worse but worst thing it could
be and of course it always
can but of course it usually
isn't because common things
are common and always at
the top of the possibilities list
except when those thoughts

arrive (as they always do)
the ones I labeled that fear
that imprinted that germ

that seed that sprouted
makes uncommon things
at the bottom of the list
rise to the top even when
the doctor says it will be
alright maybe it won't as
the doctor likely said the
same thing back then
about you after ordering
the chocolate penicillin just
before it was very very not
alright and that germ that
seed that was waiting for
my babies to be born be-
fore sprouting sprouted as

soon as the first day of
my first baby when that
common newborn yellow
that yellow sunlight cures
had me going to the dark
dark sunless place of what
if the yellow goes to her
little brain as I read that it
uncommomly can read it
in that library textbook when
I should have been cooking
dinner in a cast iron skillet
for her nursing mom and
of course it can and of
course almost never does
and didn't so then after
those 2 or 3 days of going

back to the hospital the
wounding of her tiny heel
for that drop of yellowed
blood and waiting waiting
fearing exposing as much

of her tiny surface as we
could to the yellow sun
fearing it won't work won't
be enough sun through
closed windows on cooler
than usual mid-May days
until the yellow faded from
skin and blood and felt relieved only briefly labeling
it dodged this time but
what's next and every day
ever since the thoughts
arrive (as they always do)
I label what's next and try
to return to the breath but
it is held up stopped blocked
in my throat and for the

second baby and now
over 30 years later the
first baby's first baby the
same things it just keeps
rolling on maybe different
triggers but the same labeled thoughts the same reflex
responses and you're only
as safe as your last normal
lab test or scan or office
visit and the reassurance
of those normals doesn't
last long as every day
every week every month
that passes you know
surely something else could

have cropped up crept up by
now every news story every
neighborhood and schoolyard
tale every social media post

about what happened to this
baby that toddler this or that
boy or girl crib death lumps
that were tumors stiff necks
that were meningitis hearts
stopping on soccer fields always the worst thing as it
was with you and I gasp
and cover my mouth and
hold my breath and widen
my eyes could that happen
to my kid my grandkid of
course it can and of course
it probably won't uncommon
things are uncommon but no

logic no reason no data about
common vs uncommon about
frequency and incidence or
likeliness and unlikeliness of
same place same family same
lightning strikes stops it yet
even with all that watching
and waiting every now and
then something does happen
does slip by unexpected
or expected and if expected
you see you see I told you
and if unexpected good Lord
why didn't I see that coming
you see you see now I can
add unreasonable guilt to
unreasonable fear and will
have to watch and worry
even harder the fear always
wins always demands attention and in its grip nothing
else matters except seeking
resolution relief peace every

social or workplace conver-
sation perfunctory every
interest feigned every smile
thin and weak and fake until
resolution relief peace or ex-
haustion no ability to enjoy to

experience pleasure it seems
so irresponsible so foolish to
stop worrying to stop watching
even an instant when something can slip by you so selfish
to indulge in something anything that might pause the
fear or give momentary
relief if it means letting up
even a nanosecond in the
mission to protect as Mom's
grief and sadness and fear
imprinted on me instructed
me to do unlike that parable
about the man chased by
two tigers one on the cliff
above as he clings to a
vine and the other in the
valley below waiting for him
to drop as two mice chew on
the vine when he sees and
decides to pluck the straw-
berry on the nearby ledge
and enjoy how sweet but

no such sweet berry tast-
ing or rose smelling stops
for me when something terrible may happen to those
I must guard besides seeming weak lacking courage
or strength or the selfless

urge to sacrifice self for
these young precious fragile
others as you were young
precious fragile and left un-
protected the fear the watching demands attention vigi-
lance it is up to me to pre-
vent the kind of catastrophe
that befell you except it's too

much I can't do it but also can't
not do it can't leave these little
ones unguarded can't disobey
Mom the one who planted the
seed the germ always in my
ear telling me to never let what
happened to you happen to
anyone else again not my
children not my grandchildren
but in selfish spent moments
I still want to shake off the
mission and not have it be
up to me I can't save the
world or even the little bit
of it in front of me I want
to pray as Jesus prayed
for the cup to pass but
since I am no Messiah
no Son of God I really
want the cup to pass His

will not be done I will
sweat blood shed bloody
tears if the cup will pass
to know the relief and
release of the cup passing
I know it's selfish when I
should be selfless guarding
my little ones from danger

as Mom and Dad and the
doctor did not could not
guard you but I don't want
that job it's too much Jesus
died for us so I don't have
to he carried the cross but

I carry your name in the
middle of mine except I
am not you you were not
around long enough to
know it but years after
you were gone our next-
door neighbors got a little
terrier they named Winston
with a signature bark so
unwelcomed anytime but
especially weekend wake-
up mornings but they loved
him anyway and when
he died they must have
missed him so much they
replaced him right away
with another dog that looked
the same and barked the
same they named him
Winston 2 so I can

imagine how Mom and
Dad must have missed
you so much that beauti-
ful baby I see now in pictures and 8 mm movie
reels unearthed from
basement and attic boxes
as treasures from some
pharaoh's tomb like the
one from our older brother's
5th birthday 5 months before

that Monday night with Mom's
sister holding you and Mom's
pregnant belly full of me and
how they all looked smiling
in those post-war boom and
blessing years that 5 months
and 13 days later when that
was all taken away I can
imagine them wanting to
just fill that hole as quickly
as possible to get a Donnie
2 and they didn't have to

look very far I was right
there in the cradle and
from that same pharaoh's
trove a movie of a baby
me on Mom's lap only 2
months after you were
gone and she is holding
a 3 month-old me smooth-
ing out the rumpled blanket
around me black bloused
looking far away and maybe
it was just the day or a passing mood or the poor light-
ing on those old films but
seeing it now trying to read
it now I am more convinced
it was still dark dark dark
then another one 5 months

after that and Mom is smiling
bouncing the Donnie 2.0 me
that half looked like you and
carried your whole name in
the middle of mine and with
it all the grief the sadness
the anger the unfairness

the fear that it will happen
again the same fear I saw
on Mom's face whenever
that 4th boy born 2 and a
half years later the iration-
al illogical optimistic leap
after you were gone had
croup bouts the same
fear that meant it would be

Dad who got home from
work at nighttime 9 and
would be getting up to go
back at daytime 6 but
overnight would have to
take him into the shower
steam to find his breath
while a 3 or 4 year old me
carrying your name in the
next bedroom (and every-
where) hearing the com-
motion awakened and
decided to join the action
thinking it fun to draw on
the bathroom mirror fog
the mind part of my mind
the reasonable part of my
reasoning knows it was
random unlikely uncommon

and the fact that it still
occurred doesn't make it
more likely to occur again
yet the unreasonable part
of my reasoning lives in the
world of the uncommon
mountains those dark rag-
ged cloud shrouded craggy
peaks full of frightening fore-

boding mystery with distant
lightning flashes in every
storm rather than the bright
familiar comfortably common
molehills but also wonders
how I can make it all stop
I really need it to stop

IV

Vermont Has A High Suicide Rate

at least that's
what Paul says
and he

should know,
he's a doctor
there, near Burlington

who supplements his income
with farming and
maple sugaring, and

makes the kind
of money in
twelve months that

a megalopolitan madman
might go through
in two, and lives

more simply than simple,
can go
to work with

muddy boots, has
a fine beard,
and is happy.

Why, I ask
in a place
that means green

mountain, where what
look like clouds
actually are,

and the land
is the way,
not in the

way, of life
are the people
killing themselves?

It's the winters,
Paul says,
people can get

crazy when it's
so cold
so long.

Hover Craft

Hair grown back now, always wanted but
critical starting pre-K; backpack straps curve
over shoulders and cross collar bones that
only six months ago knobbed out of loose
gowns in cold onc unit rooms now unseen
under shirt and needless jacket in still-summer
September; no books packed yet, just 10:30
snack—half sandwich on whole wheat chick
pea mash medium for maitake powder magic,
organic juice box chaser, and the teacher—

Miss Lindsay or Kristen—barely 28 with kindly
smile but no idea they were handing off two years
living scan to scan when every headache is
alarm and every smile scrutinized to see both
mouth sides rise, no idea she had barely been
out of their sight that whole time except weekday
workdays for him and those short spells of light-
sleep nights for both until the monitor pinch
hitting out of attic retirement buried breathing
noise with crackle and hiss and one of them
would be up, doorway gazing, bedside lurking
or sometimes floor quilt all-nighting, but

after the "all clear" and "start living" advice
the four hours MWF mornings might work
with rules: Bus stop corner curbside? One
more germ-swap-athon when the classroom
and playground meant too many already? And
all those stops stretching a car's 2 miles and
5 minutes to half an hour plus? Plus risk motion
sick too mixed with other dizzy queasy makers
and too much like the PICC port times? No. We
drive, last-minute drop-off and come-early pickup just in case, just in case; and in between the
phone always on, Fur Elise ring tone set high,

avoid tree-alee back roads, parks, the frozen-
food aisle and every other dead cell spot and
never forget to re-charge every overnight.

Division of labor

College kid had the stiff neck and temp.

Girlfriend insisted on the hospital.

ER tech caught him when he crumped.

ER doc saw the rash and bolused the meds.

Anesthesia did the LP.

Micro saw the gram-negative diplos.

Parents got the wee hours nightmare call.

Records said he'd been immunized.

Easy hows got answered; impossible whys not.

ICU doc made losing fingers the best hope.

Respiratory noted no vent override.

Uncle came from out of town.

Employee health prophylaxed exposees.

Papers picked up the story.

Risk manager pored over ER chart.

Dorm-mates and lab partners packed Student Health.

Neurologist noted all quiet north of neck.

ICU nurse agreed it looked like sleep.

Vent withdrew.

Laundry picked up gowns.

Housekeeping bleached room.

heart doctor father

Ron speaks softly about
Paul stepping up to
take one for the team
germ cell hard ball
to the sternum, deadly exception
to prove the rule that
most chest pain in young men is
reflux or intercostal tension

who listened quietly for
25 years to bruits over arteries
that earned yellow stripes
with fat and tobacco, now
hears his own heart click,
split, snap as the surgeon
describes stripping tumor
off innocent pericardium

who just a week before
heard Paul's marriage and
law school plans but
now they discuss
Indiana chemo wizards
harvesting sperm before
sterilizing shots of
platinum, hair loss and
maybe die in raw
words that echo off
late night stark light
kitchen tile

who always chirped "karma"
when bad things happened but is
reduced to whispers and
knocked to his knees by
this very bad thing his
emotions scattered

like shards of the fractured
illusion that parents will
always be able to
protect their children and
physician-parents protect them
even better

who finds in the rubble
his estranged Catholic
grade school God, pushing up
through layers of rational rejection
and years of agnostic distance
not friends again exactly, but
talking, sharing stories of
blameless suffering sons

44

and gone after only
one year of the
colon-to-liver
usual yellow alacrity

husband and daughters
stand straight, serene, and smiling
in the receiving line
without pharmacy brain buzz
they welcome other addled 44's to
"the celebration of her rebirth"
saying, "she's an angel now"
and soberly mean every word
as clear-eyed and radiant as
she ever was

looking so all right they
give us space
to indulge self
they comfort our red
swollen eyes not
quite ready to see her or us
with wings and harps at
44

we scramble for meaning and
pretend to find some as
we hiccup around the wake
promising to grab gusto since
life is short when
what we really want are
answers
data

unwilling to accept
random circumstance
we strain to see

something different about her
in genes
or diet
or swallowed stress

something we don't have
or don't do
or won't ever do again

something that will let us
sleep tonight and
work tomorrow
feeling safe at
44

Plans

How old was she?
53; 54 maybe.
our age
two girls
on the team

And how long ago
was she diagnosed?

Year and a half. I know
that one exactly because
playoffs start in two
weeks, and she was at
last year's wigged and
luminous in the bleachers
after six chemo months, but by

finals the wig was off and
in her gray-red pan-scalp
corkscrew stubble she
bubbled over as ever about
impossible 3-pointers
harassing refs over bad calls
missed fouls and traveling
can't you see she
traveled!

And when did they find
the effusion? The mets?

Don't know. Nor do I
know how much of
Thoreau's quiet
desperation she hid
at Seniors Day just
last week under
eye sparkle, smile, and

halting gushes about our
chances at Districts, or
what it took to pick

the garage ceiling 1X6
decide on
bathrobe belt, find
right-height chair, unlike

brash bullet or
impulse pill gulp—
plans
preparation
choices
time to reverse

How old did you say?

Racing

She asked why the ex-
terminator bills went into
the miscellaneous file not
"paid invoices" with the
landscaper and township
sewer charges so after
the briefest pause to won-

der whether those sprays
and powders to kill ants
yellow jackets and stink
bugs might have played
any part in why they were
doing this now he tried to
explain the difference be-

tween recurring budget-
ed expenses vs more oc-
casional stuff such as pest
control but then she asked
why the cell phone carrier
wasn't in paid invoices too
so he laid out his logic of

including those with water
and electric as "utilities . . .
you know, like in Mono-
poly?" but when her look
glazed over he acted as
if it was the newness of
what he had to teach

and she had to learn not
why he had to teach it
and she had to learn it
now as they told him it
could be as short as

months and with luck
a year or more so he

knew he was racing not
just what was in back
he had hoped was just
disc pain until the MRI
said no then the hunt
for where it started that
lit up lungs and brain

but also the start of the
poisons and radiating
fatigue they said to ex-
pect plus between bone
burn and fear the steep
sleep hill so he knew
he had to get her up

to speed fast but when
he tried to break her
faraway stare with
"this is just my system
you can make your own"
she said, "no, that's OK,
keep going, I'll get it."

The Vonnegut letter

hadn't yet been published when Tommy
was the first in our class to pass at 45
and we assumed his rectal exception
only proved our invulnerable rule so
it was safe to keep working watching
school shows soccer games saving
tuitions dreaming a 401K future that
at 20 past 45 is here and now since

New Year's we've seen Rob's robot
bypass reboot after years of untend-
ed belly bulge Hank's pancreas after
months of unheeded bellyalgia Jack's
stroke after unwatched warfarin only a
few fluttering weeks and unfathomably
Billy found chair slumped already hard
as his run-route streets and cold as his
unfinished rice-bean bowl and suddenly
the new rule has *in* fleeing *vulnerable*
and us all out there getting mowed down
left and right and left to wonder who'll be

next which blood-tinged something lump
finger tingle will blossom to badness and
what to do when this must-have book of
letters arrives fanning my former Titan
Rosewater Slaughterhouse affection so
while one of us pledges to schedule overdue labs scope calcium score and another
to tend his belly with the meal and move-
ment measures that failed poor Billy I am

reading and rereading what Kurt wrote
home in '45 post POW release about what
strafing fire-bombing and even delousing
shower shock did to captured comrades

and Dresden's quarter million saying over
and over "Many men died ... but I didn't ...
not me" as I say now it seems every other
week invoking similar Fortune smiles or
simpler dumb luck.

Four perfect quarters

when I lost the green ash twelve
summers ago you came into the yard
with a saw and a deal—
for half the haul you'd
cut it all into ready rounds
and teach me to maul split, to
aim for the inviting cleft
let tool and gravity do the work
breathe, bend knees, relish

the way the four quarters fall apart, the look
and smell of startled heartwood
the flat dull ring of a thrown log on its
partners, like tumbling children's blocks
a siren song that always called you back
to my yard or kept you in yours
working other hauls from other deals

I don't remember when I stopped
hearing your hammer or smelling
your November smoke or knew about the
six heme grams, ten sigmoid inches
forty-seven pounds you lost, and
thousands of portal triads sliced
microtome thin, or how long since the

stiff-suited day I walked yard to yard past
your pile—a blue tarp capped peak above
border tangle of honeysuckle and wild rose
—to sit inside a circle of cakes with dew
beads slipping off polished shoes and tell
stories stacked tall enough to last many winters

but wish you could have seen me with
my own saw after the May storm took
the black walnut by the fence, or been lured
today by the claves clack under a July cicada

sun to watch me work the few rounds I hid
from millers and carvers, or sweat with
me over that stuck-wedge stubborn

or been home to see the four perfect
quarters I laid next to your dwindle of
parched gray oak, to admire the way the cut
bared the grain, pointing like a candle flame,
like church steeple, the light brown almost
yellow, the dark almost violet; you would have
warned me to keep on my gloves, that the wet
bark would stain my hands

the stroke in 111A

is somebody's uncle
who was part of
safe warm week-over friday night
visits, making chuckling kitchen din
over coffee and coffee cake
while nephew half-watched half-dreamed
77 sunset strip
on the living room floor

is somebody's father
who watched his daughter's
first birthday through the
gray square of an old
super-eight, blinding everyone
with the floodlight rack he
balanced in one hand while
motioning with the other to
move the cake closer
closer to the baby

is somebody's husband
who took his wife to
atlantic city after the war
and charted a sunny future
in sand finger doodles
when hope bubbled like lava
out of the victory volcano

is getting orders to "go"
so he goes with
loose gown flapping like
motorcade flags and
leads a paretic parade of
trailing tethering tubing
to the bathroom
pulling out balloon-and-all foley
felling i.v. pole

falling
into a tube-spill puddle that
spreads red from sliced-scalp-drip as

the family walks in
nephew daughter wife who will
crash vision against memory
like cymbals and
cover their ears

Maple Grove

is the specimen red alee along the
long curving driveway that ends at
the colonial brick portico to the final-
move final-movers invited into a walled
city where walker wheels roll on hallway
highways from the neighborhoods of
Independence and Assisted to in-house
hair appointments and convenience
shopping and dinner and Wednesday
scrabble and any-time cards and hoped-
for never or no time soon stretcher-
wheeled rides to Skilled where so many
go and so few return and after Thursday
night's talk on neuron-stretching crosswords
and cryptograms a renamed game room
the "Brain Gym at the

Grove"

is E.R. code for the soft SNF admission for
every urine cloud or cough or ventricular
sputter, sometimes personified as when
nurse or tech or doc comes cussing out of
Room 6 with "Getting a line to run in a
Grover is like sticking a twig" or "They have
O2 there and meds go through PEGs so why
not just let them stay and go quietly at the

Grove"

was the native sugar swamp silver and red
hardwood stand that stood tall with oak poplar
sweetgum ash before the developer aimed for
their orange spray-painted X-marked-hearts-
spots and the excavator clawed at what was
left of their stiff drying xylem trunks and roots
clearing them and the post-glacial gray green

serpentine rocks for the cinder block stacks of
would-be underground garage full of even-
spaced white lines some weak ankles and grips
and failing eyes and forgotten directions might
turn into permanent parking until the hearse
and tow truck come and it all starts again
for a new someone moving to

Maple Grove.

Refusing Ginkgo

when my memory falters
I want nothing to spare ACH
let it tumble into a synaptic cleft
scream in the abyss
plop into the receptor jaws of hungry
cholinesterase, and be eaten alive

no Vitamin E
I want oxidative damage to
run wild, pick off temporal lobe
neurons, take shots at 1992 when
I thought dizzy ringing
was acoustic neuroma

I look forward to forgetting
years of money–children–work–worry
encouraged that I might be able to
erase the day's tapes of bad decisions that
replay nightly on a 0330 ceiling

to be like Nursing Home Sal
in his stained and dried-rice grained pants
who should know my name yet
won't say it most days but when dinner is
under his nose will smile between
shaky-handed forkfuls

just wheel me outside sometimes
in mid June on the
first firefly night, then
late July when the cicada clicks start
early September for the first cool wind
and the winding down crickets
end October when peak gold maple leaves
dance before dropping

in November to December
when the fifteen brown shades earth is
quiet before snow
and again in January
after a blizzard blanket lays
new and unplowed
and one last April time when
melt-water lifts mud and crocus heads
so I can see it hear it smell it
feel it all for the first time

Brunch at Judy's

Café means aiming for the no-wait
window between 9 and 1030 Mass-
end peaks but after that a drive-by
sighting of no outdoor crowd says
safe to park though in chilly or wet
weather they line up inside along

white bead board-bordered vestibule
walls but tables still turn over fast
except today when the door opens and
nothing but cold air arrives for so long
it announces a parade first front wheels
and metal poles then whole walker like

single movie film frames each a new
position advancing slowly to hostess
stand the lateish-50's children trailing
and even without looking and certainly
not staring it's hard not to notice the
fixed face gray skin empty stare the
slowness of everything except the flap
flap flapping of hands trying to rest on

front handlebars a shaky defense
against the floor's pull but Judy and her
girls so sweet and everyone on queue
saying with looking-away looks sure seat
them first and not 5 minutes after the 5

minutes it takes them to settle down they
are up again and doubtless diuretic-driven
to rest room and while they're gone it seems
so much trouble a couple of eggs scrambled
in a different pan to be bobbled on a different

fork and fall under a different chair than
at home though maybe a morning outing

works better for the kids eating time off
the time-together attention clock mostly
task-related talk and tasks to load him

drive to Judy's pro-cess in sit rise to go to
go come back sit read menu ("What looks
good? Do you want bacon with that? What
about home fries?") order wait eat pay pro-
cess out drive back unload so much better

than an evening sit against the Afghan throw
knit by grandma-someone during the Korean
War and not washed since Watergate that
always slides down on the slick slip-cover sofa
back half-talking over high-dB background

Lawrence Welk rerun on floor console TV half-
angry he insists on keeping the house living alone
and good Lord still driving and half-relieved he
keeps the house lives alone 'cause good Lord do

you really want him with you but after doing the
early duty at Judy's the evening will be ahhhhh!
free for maybe later-time-zone big screen any-ball
or wildebeest migrating thunder or streaming
something anything on demand or dinner out
or maybe not but

our table is ready.

Sal doesn't shake

but he shuffles
trunk hunched
jaw dropped
arms swing-less and
stiff at sides
can't turn on a dime
but must stutter step
around a quarter's corners

parks n' lakes
parkson, parkinson
little lake strokes or
depression are the
doctor's three maybes he
fishes for and finally finds
when kind questions
come in company

but no help yet from
dope, dope-a-mean
I mean I mean

at poker
Sal doesn't shake
or shuffle or deal
but folds with
three-of-a-kind
parks lakes depression

at the park where
he shuffle-walks along the
row of queen anne's
lace he notices tiny
purple petals in the slight
depression at the centers;
a striking violet speck in an

otherwise ocean of flower-head
white which others
moving more
quickly easily
might miss

When the crash cart

hit the tray table blocking the door
seven wish-well cards domino
tumbled and a red ribbon tail escaped
its sandbag berth then floated and
dipped as its balloon head tapped
the ceiling by the window

we stared as the monitor's green
line sputtered spikes settled into
R-row order and you glared through
the clearing hair singe smoke,
through the thicker haze of your
reasonable question given the
rib crush heart bruise
lung leak liver lac
and his 79 years, except that

five days before he was loading
logs in the bed of an old pickup that
slipped out of Park so often they
usually blocked the wheels, but
with the right load and the right
driveway pitch it rolled back
over wedges and flannel shirt, so
we'll give him that one; but now

one son, two daughters, an ex-
wife and the respiratory tech
nephew know we can't wean
the vent, the kidneys are
keeping creatinine and he's not
waking up even off-azepam, so
if family agrees and policy permits the
next time we'll stay off the chest, let
pupils drift to iris edges where
they stop as dented disks and
corneas steel to cotton wisps till

no reflex blink breaks his stare up
to where the balloon in ambient
indoor wind still knocks near the
closed window and looks out over
the mixed hardwood canopy beyond
the north wing

"when they took the IV out"

she said from the hospice
room loveseat moving the
red and yellow floral quilt
from behind her to the
armrest wondering when
it was last washed and

"why is this room so hot"

recalling his shivers hours
earlier when whether pur-
poseful or reflex he pulled
covers to chin with sinew
shrunken arms because it
wasn't the limb dwindle to
spider leg spindles or the
white chest CT swirl pum-
meling left lower lobe like
hurricane season squalls
might pound cowering
coasts and the time I found

her on a chilly ICU lounge
loveseat after his bypass
just awakened hair tousled
pointing out frayed fabric
under the armchair she
saw lying down we agreed
he'd dodged one but knew
more would come and her

"who still smokes after heart surgery"

painfully prophetic only two
years post LAD reboot not
even after they agreed to
transfer setting off that fire-

drill hour of canceled orders
a labored change from gown
gray print to tracksuit blue and
a rushed stuffed belongings
bag later she looks at his sleeping or narcotized haze his grim-
ace-free face they assure her
means no pain listening for the
end-near breaths they said
will come thinking when the

CABG IVs went in it was like
game-on luer lock and load
and when they came out
uncork the bubbly a victory
parade down Main (with a
pharmacy stop) before home
bed and blanket but this time

"when they took the IV out"

ginger ale flat fizz a will-we
even-make-it-there ambu-
ance ride to a towel-thrown-
in loveseat vigil by armrest-
draped alien quilt washed
who knows when awaiting
real or seeming sleep transfer to some other where

Buddy's final colors

Buddy lay down in blue
lay down
laid out
in blue
powder pants
navy blazer
as if heaven might be
a Boardwalk stroll on a
May-blue cool night

while Agnes spins on the word
"aspiration"
and how his
can't cough can't swallow stroke
and a blue-nail pneumonia
cancelled her red-hearted hope

she stares at his fingers sticking out of
white cuffs like sticks,
like storm-grounded twig-hands
colored brown to cover
blown IV blotch
and remembers how she pictured this
watching him sleep in his Unit bed
except now
no tubes
no O2 hiss
no gown askew, half covering
the Foley-strapped thigh
no bronchial gurgle rattle

only the white satiny coffin fluff
and the priest in basic black
circling through gray rising smoke
chanting and stepping in time to the
censer's clink clink

and the slacks and coat
closet crisp after
nine months under
dry cleaner plastic
ready for one more
Jersey junket,
Agnes hoping even
as he slipped because
white light tunnel trips
can be round

but getting a
no-code
one way
lay down
in blue

Mary Elise believes

the dead return as cardinals, told
her kids their pop-pop had
come back scarlet feathers and travel
song to the open window ledge.   I

didn't have this in mind when
Sal went from soon to
any day and neurofibril tangles
kept shutting down lights and
shorting switches till the last two
weeks he never even opened his
eyes, and gape-mouthed Cheyne
Stokes' snores dried his palate
shiny red, or

even think of it the day
before when nettle
bed digging almost
buried a fallen fledgling,
spotty feathered fuzz trying to
roll upright, eyes closed, mouth
open wanting something
in a mother's beak, with the
dusky red female two branches up
in the honeysuckle understory, her
short shrill sharp chirps till   I

remembered the empty
robin's nest under the deck and
wondered if a mother's wings
would neglect a baby in a
foreign bird bed as they would one
human handled, so without touching   I

shoveled dirt, felled nettles and
hatchling into nest, treed it and the next
morning Sal was gone.   I

don't remember opening any
windows but so often since
I've seen the blood red male—first
in the black walnut by the fence, next
atop the white mulberry near the
swings, every time singing
coming closer

In Vince's dream

he and Sam were
walking
W A L K I N G !

       before Vince's sugar legs
       gave surgeons a blue toe inch
       and they took two cold feet
       then whittled him up
       to his knees where phantoms floated
       over wheelchair rests

they met at the corner of
Westfield and Laurel
shook hands and were
really glad to see each other

       before time disappeared in Sam's
       Lewy Body land where
       dysarthric stiff made smile shrink
       and forgetting included
       step right lift left

they planned their weekly
card game with John
George and Al, my place
or yours, doesn't matter

       before Vince's mystery liver scars
       needing weekly taps sent him
       begging for the shunt he once refused
       and the x-ray dye knocked his
       kidneys and him down a last time

said see ya Tuesday night
and walked away
W A L K ED away!
down Laurel

up Westfield

before Sam's urosepsis bought him
supra-pubic and G-tubes and
good God, he could strong heart
this one a long time

after Vince's dignity directive
let his respirations slip to
one   two   a minute
a long lip rattling sigh
out of a closed eye poker face said
callin' it, boys
read 'em and weep

Dressed for dinner

When the lockdown shut down
the dining room and kitchen
staff temporarily started bringing meals to residents' apart-
ments she got out of the habit
of getting out of her nightgown
all day but when the visiting OT
saw this she called her daughter
with a depression concern

(of course I'm depressed who
wouldn't be 96 and trapped in
here all these months can't see
you or my grandchildren or
great-grandchildren can't go to
pokeno or dinner) and while

both OT and daughter tried
pep talks hang in there you'll
get your first shot in a week
and your second 4 weeks after
that and after that things will
open up you'll see you'll see

your family go back to dining
room meals the community
administrator wanted a PCP
discussion about adding meds
and pushing pushing a move
out of independent into assisted
living where there was more
daily interaction with staff
prompting another in a series
of come-to-Jesus daughter talks

(if you don't get yourself up and
dressed and ready for the day

they will think you can't take
care of yourself and won't let
you stay in this apartment)
and another in a series of pre-
dictable fired back responses

(I'm not moving they just want
more of my money well they're
not going to get it they want me
to get dressed to eat dinner in
my room I'll get dressed) mean-

while on every OT phone pic her
legs swelled more and on every
phone call her breathing and
chat time shortened as the
breathing room between
aortic valve leaflets thinned
then diuretic dose tweaks
kidney filter rate checks chest
xrays to find failure fluid calf
sonograms to rule out clot

(more drugs and tests always
more drugs and tests just because I have good insurance)

and the dining room re-opened
and re-closed and re-opened
tracking virus case counts but
when the OT visited and saw
pills spilled on the floor the administrator said at least you
have to let us manage that so

that was the compromise every
morning at 8 a door knock and
meds delivered and OK to still
be nightgowned at that hour

until that morning she didn't
answer and they found her on

the floor by her bed dressed in
gray wool pants pink crew-
neck top and the white sweater
the grandkids got her last Christmas the last time they were all
together pre-demic they guessed
it probably happened the night
before getting ready to go to or
just coming back from dinner.

Arrived

as doctor-son to weekly visit the one
grilling nurses on leg swells and missed
meds the other kneeling chair-side in the
dayroom corner she nodding at phone pix
of grands and great-grands speaking only
to ask PLEASE let me go home and after my
3rd THIS is your home closing her eyes as if
streaming the unimaginable everything
seen loved feared mourned in all but 3
weeks of 99 years shaking her head as if
thinking No not this then 10 hours later

standing bedside in 2AM quiet she lying
so still eyes closed jaw dropped till angel
nurse knew to prop towel-roll under chin
skin still so warm Were they sure? check
radial carotid Is that bounding pounding
hers or mine? Finally lift eyelids shine
phone light at pupils nothing nothing No
not this then 2 nights later

as dreamer to a forest floor nest with one
squawky hawk fledge in cracked shell cap
but sensing fearing its mother watched
angrily nearby I tried to run but fell in stiff-
legged panic then woke shaken but shook
it off and found a web blurb on dream
hawks as messengers then 5 days later

as doctor to a work desk still dream
addled window staring still stuck on
how her closed casket wish had firmly
fixed that last visit vision when the red
tail arrived on the fence by the yew row
so I moved to get a closer look maybe
click a phone pic hear a message from
home then a heartbeat later
she took off.

V

I carry your name (b)

which brings me to
you it started with you
and now 68 years after
that germ that seed was
implanted and waiting to
sprout and sprouted 31
years later and 35 years
after that first sprouting
it is still alive still growing
with gnarly twisted trunks
and branches I need to see
how I can make it stop and
I believe it has to start with

you maybe I could make
it stop by imagining
or even knowing you are
OK now that even though
it hurt you and them in the
moment and you were so
afraid in Mom's arms where
you had always been so safe
and they were so sad to see
you go and then afraid that
what happened to you could
happen to our older brother
or to me still cradle-bound
or to the ones that came
after me and now I am so
afraid that what happened
to you could happen to my
little ones or later to my
little ones' little ones maybe

in those times when we sus-
pend the rational and like to
think about ideas such as

heaven and reunion maybe
I can find relief and release
imagining Mom and Dad
back with you (and maybe
the uncle is there too and
maybe he can tell Mom
that I really did spend
some time at his house
in diapers back then but
if she still denies or doesn't
remember don't push it if
she is happy now let it be)

so because I've come to
believe that it started with
you maybe I've now come
to believe I can end it through
you too I've carried your name
all these years so I come to
you with a twist on Juliet's
question about a name and
a rose she suggested were
arbitrary labels a rose would
smell as sweet no matter
what we called it so perhaps
even less meaning in a middle name would my life have
smelled more sweet without
the weight and the sadness
and the fear in the middle
of my name given to honor
and preserve your memory
these middle names that
are so often optional filling

out forms they want your
last they want your first
name and there's a spot
for a middle or just an

initial a single letter that
stands for something but
so often isn't asterisked
not a required field ex-
cept on documents that
announce and confirm
who you really are it's
staring at you from your
drivers license next to
your picture your eye
color hair color that half
looks like yours the name
you write when signing
those DMV forms no
escaping it part of who
you are added 6 weeks
after birth and 13 days
after you were gone at the
chrism cross anointing
and holy water sprinkling
and later to an amended
birth certificate so it's no
use the name is now mine
to carry and with it all the
sadness and grief and
fear the fear always the

fear but I want to believe
that if I bring you back
somehow bring you back
as that living breathing at
least for two years living
breathing joyful playful
trickster boy that looked
half like me and half like
the one that came after
me that if I bring back
the you that was alive
before there was a you

that departed and caused
the sadness and grief and
fear maybe the sadness
and grief and fear will

ease maybe lift though
if I had to make a deal
if this had to be transac-
tional I would keep the
sadness and grief and
the memory of that sweet
little boy the rose smelling
as sweet whether the name
is your first or my middle
keep those if I could lose
the fear the living on high
alert every second every
minute every hour every
day perched on that high
ridge watching watching
waiting for the worst things

the dark side the uncom-
mon mountains the 2nd
3rd 4th lightning strikes
but even though that is
where I have learned to
live it is not a life there
is no room for joy when
you're always afraid but
how can you stop watch-
ing how can you stop cry-
ing wolf when you know
one of these times maybe
the next time it will be the
wolf and when it isn't you
feel relieved but not long
because you know the
next time yes the next

time that will be the one
unless I watch and protect
except I have to make it

stop for the very keep it
real reason that I can't
protect any lives if I don't
have a life myself so I
am coming to you for
help to ease it lift it maybe even make it go away
I want to believe that we
pushed you away to avoid
the sadness and now we
need to bring you back
there is enough sadness
and fear about what does
happen about what has
happened but to spend
limited and precious time
and attention on what
is possible but unlikely
only because what was
possible and unlikely did
happen once to you and
once and maybe again
to many others like you
doesn't make it any
more likely to happen to
someone anyone else
that thinking has to end
and of course you can't

no one can change what
has happened but bring-
ing you back to life in attention in thoughts in remembering the joy you
were the joy you brought

at least may help offset
balance the sadness of
losing you then missing
you and hopefully help
manage the fear left in its
wake of course I can't be
sure but feel strongly that
I ignore you push away
thoughts of sadness and
fear because of what hap-
pened to you at my peril
feel maybe even you don't
like being ignored and that

if I continue to try to ignore
you maybe you will try to
get my attention by mak-
ing me afraid so maybe
if I start paying you more
attention you will quiet
down you will change the
message to something
like hey what happened
was awful and really
scary for me and then
awful and really sad
for all of you and now
really scary for you but
also really uncommon
and you know what
they say about uncom-
mon things but also be-
cause it happened to
me and I took one for
the team maybe you
will be OK and your
children and grandchild-
ren will be OK and of
course thinking that way

may be just as crazy as
the watching and waiting
but inside that thought
a new thought not the
thoughts that arrive (as
they always do) that I
label fear and what's
next a new thought I
can label relief and
release so I am lean-

ing into you bringing
you back keeping your
memory alive the way
it was kept alive with
the middle name I carry
and celebrating you cel-
ebrating the two years
you lived and did all the
things we can see you
doing in pictures and
films and all the things
we heard about you do-
ing in stories Dad would
tell and sometimes even
Mom would tell when that
faraway look might briefly
pass that mood briefly lift
like the time you relocated
what was in your diaper
to the ashtray so every-
one would think it was
one of Dad's cigars by
look and smell or the
time you rocked my cra-
dle till it fell over the
way you still rock my
sleep and that maybe
with all that intentional

attention you won't need
to get my attention by
making me afraid we

can certainly still feel
sad that we never got
the chance to know you
grown up but we can
move past sadness and
regret and remember the
time you did spend with us
because now we are bring-
ing you back so we won't
have to be afraid anymore
maybe you will tell me it's
OK to be careful but not
to overdo overdose that
caution and care-taking
and careful-being are OK
but being driven and con-
trolled by fear every day
not OK not healthy and
not sustainable although I

promise that carrying your
name means I will never
forget and shouldn't forget
like the Viet Nam PTSD
vet who doesn't want to
lose his nightmares and
be disloyal to the memo-
ries of those he lost so
maybe I would be dis-
loyal to you or to those
babies I fear for how can
I ignore worrying and stop
watching when it might
mean I don't care as
much I'm not taking my

responsibility responsibly
enough so maybe I will

keep the waking night-
mares as living memory
of you and what it did to
our parents and us and
me but maybe channel
it some other way keep
it integrate what I have
not been able to and
probably cannot and
probably should not e-
liminate but maybe em-
brace new thoughts ar-
riving (as I hope they
will) I can label release
and relief maybe I can

understand my steeping
in fear now my inability to
climb out or bounce back
now was because Mom
was absent for a time not
there to comfort me and
and though the worst
trauma is inflicted by the
ones supposed to protect
us Mom didn't mean it
couldn't help not being
there then I understand
now and forgive her so

I carry your name I have
carried it all but 6 weeks
of my life and with it the
sadness and grief the
anger and fear so now
what do I do with that the

thought that arrives (as it
always does) I label mem-
ory and sadness and grief
and fear and return to the
breath renewing the breath
you lost breathing for you
breathing you alive again
but I also label it the joy
we need to remember too
as I keep following the
breath keep breathing
for you into you into your
first name the one I carry
in my middle and today

into your birthday breathing
alive a different response a
more reasoning response
about common things that
don't have to become the
uncommon horrible things
but with your help I will
deal with whatever comes
and not expect the uncom-
mon every time and know
I can be angry and sad
and frustrated and even
afraid but whatever hap-
pened and happens was
not and is not my job to
watch and wait the scout
up on the ridge can come
down and re-join the family

and you might want to know
or maybe you can see from
up there or wherever after
is and you are that the babies
I felt charged to protect your

nieces have grown in wis-
dom and light I never wanted that fear to land on them
that seed that germ to get
planted in them and later
to sprout but I can't shield
them from the world we
worked so hard to launch
them into and the one
that is a mother now her-
self has already seen it
and felt it from friends
that have lost little ones
the way Mom and Dad
lost you little Donnies

happening every day
somewhere those horrible
uncommon things arrive
(as they always do) but
how do we label them
what do we label them
the words limp the met-
aphors don't come close
the saddest sad we can
imagine a sadness so
unspeakably sad so hard
so deep like a well you
drop a coin into to wish
the sadness and fear
away but all you hear
is air rubbing against
metal dropping down
and down and down
but never the plunk
splash of water a wound
so fresh the tissue over
it so thin thin as a tissue
and while I would take a

wound that opens and
bleeds again when you
scratch it this one starts
to ooze blood with just
the memory just with
thoughts that arrive (as

they always do) and the
one with the baby of her
own tells one grief-struck
friend-mother that the
sadness is unimaginable
but imagined to be unbear-
able and yet they must bear
it they have other babies to
look after the way Mom
and Dad had to bear it to
look after our older brother
and me and the babies born
of optimism that came after
me but the only way to honor
her friend's loss is to hug her
own baby a little tighter than
before to label it the saddest
of sadnesses and return to

the breath and the other
grown baby asked me to
deliver this message to you
on your birthday "Donnie you
are a sweet spirit. We promise to celebrate you today
and every day. Comfort my
Popsie now... Now we will
keep you close because your
spirit is always alive! We are
spiritual beings who have human experiences, some longer than others." the thoughts

still arrive (as they always
do) but we can't live being
so afraid so maybe we just
label them "Donnie" and remember you and look at
your pictures whenever we
can and at your name I
carry I see in mail my name
with your name or the initial
that stands for your name on
license forms credit card apps
passport renewals in the middle of my name in the middle
of who I am announcing to
any and all who see it stone-
faced DMV staff and customs
officers and post office passport picture clicking clerks this
is who I am I can remember
the love and the joy before
the sadness and weight and
fear and hold onto the ones
still here more tightly than
ever and try as I can to re-

turn to the breath as the
thoughts arrive the ones
labeled sadness and fear
I can't erase but also joy
and thanks there in the
middle of who I am the
the first two unable to dis-
place the second instead
dancing as four as two as
one inside me as I follow
my breath to be a better
reader reading today and

saying Happy Birthday
Donnie 67 years overdue

so sorry it has taken me
so long so sorry we have
not kept this date more
forward in thoughts and
memory every now and
then growing up Mom or
Dad would realize it was
December 2nd and say
"today Donnie would have
been __" and then silence
and those faraway looks
so sorry now I did not ask
more questions but sens-
ing the silence and the
looks were self-medicating
self-soothing a way to keep
from opening that tissue-
thin wound I let it be but

now I am not letting you
be not letting the dark-
ness the shadow of that
night that has followed me
attached to your name I
carry in the middle of mine
not letting that shadow ob-
scure what I see not letting
the silence drown out what I
hear your name and mine together my whole life from 6
weeks on knowing now it can
speak a different message
can speak inside the fear
saying that what happened
to you can happen again to
any baby in any generation
but doesn't have to and is
actually unlikely to uncommon things are uncommon

so I live with dance with
breathe with and through
the fear and with your help
see that it isn't my job to
make sure this doesn't
happen to anyone else in
our family ever again be-
cause I see now that re-
leasing the fear follows
bringing you back in mem-
ory and pictures and con-
versations and thoughts
to lean into what happen-
ed to label it sadness then
get past it (never over
it) as Mom and Dad had
to get past it (never over
it) to take care of our older brother and me who
were still alive and vul-
nerable and at risk but
alive and needing feed-
ing and rumpled blankets
smoothed even if her blouse
was black and have the con-
fidence the optimism to have

more children even though
the very next one had the
same croupy cough the
work to breathe that took
you to know how afraid
they must've been but
he survived and they sur-
vived and so do we and
promise every time there
is a lifting a reprieve a
pause a time when the
fear starts to dissolve as

a fog disperses after the
sun rises as the fog on
the bathroom mirror clear-
ed when Dad opened the

door and the one after me
was breathing better and
able to go back to sleep
and I could go back to sleep
and Mom and Dad could go
back to sleep but while Dad
stole enough to carry him
through the next day's work
Mom probably stared wide-
eyed the rest of the night
listening for his breathing
maybe remembering your
breathing always returning
to the breath so maybe you
were there helping us and
all around us always ready
to help from wherever after
is and you are now so to-

day December 2nd and
from now on every Decem-
ber 2nd we will never forget
your birthday and that day
that night April 7th never
forget either maybe we
can call them Donnie-Days
D-Days the December day
you arrived washed out of
an amniotic ocean onto
Mom's belly beach and the
April day you arrived on a
cloud beach after a harrow-
ing passage through choppy
seas but once arrived there

wherever after is there were
no more attacks and you
were able to settle in and
start the job of watching
out for us and all we needed to do was see you notice
you attend to you now and

whenever thoughts of you
arrive (as they always did
and now they always will)
we will label them the
joy you were alive and
the joy you are now alive
in memory and the joy
and comfort you are now
alive in our rescue and
return to the breath and
quiet myself to hear you
say I don't have to do
this alone you are with
me always all I have to do
is notice and look at my
name with your name in
the middle of mine in the
middle of who I am and
maybe start by saying
happy birthday much
belated and just in time.

VI

compline

may our cells always
know their boundaries, our

hearts know no
failure and only
break for love and

no other brokenness that
doesn't mend, may

our nerves keep their
coats and never
tangle or fray, may

there be no self and
non-self confusion, no

confusion that doesn't
clear, no sadness that
doesn't lift, and as

for the coming of
what must certainly
come let it be like the

clock spring's final
unfurl, the soundless

release of October
Glory red maple leaf
stem from limb before

soft landing and a
future in humus, the

the slim slip of
orange sun arc beneath
the horizon edge of

western water, the
last Venus twinkle before

the yellow and
blue wash out of
dawn.

my umbilicus

reminds me that
once I was
a diver floating
in an ocean inside
a muscle cave
life-lined to
the blood-floor
by a pulsing cord

till the cave walls
shook and rumbled
and finally collapsed
squeezing me out
into a dry world
shivering and gasping
on a cold shoreline
where my tether was
cut and withered

saved when awakening
bowel-lung brewed blood
from soil and air
and rooted me there
where I grew
and grew to wonder

what's next when
this clay world
swallows my clay parts
will some other part
now sleeping
rouse, throw out
a line and
hook me into
what world
beyond stars

Permissions

"Vermont Has A High Suicide Rate": Reproduced with permission from the *Annals of Internal Medicine*. 1986.104(4):592. Copyright © (1986) American College of Physicians. All rights reserved.

"Hover Craft": Reproduced with permission from the *Journal of the American Medical Association*. 2008.300(18):2100. Copyright © (2008) American Medical Association. All rights reserved.

"heart doctor father": Reproduced with permission from the *Journal of the American Medical Association*. 1999.281(8):684. Copyright © (1999) American Medical Association. All rights reserved.

"44': Reproduced with permission from the *Journal of the American Medical Association*. 1997.277(12):943. Copyright © (1997) American Medical Association. All rights reserved.

"The Vonnegut letter": Reproduced with permission from the *Journal of the American Medical Association*. 2018.320(15):1606. Copyright © (2018) American Medical Association. All rights reserved.

"Four perfect quarters": Reproduced with permission from the *Journal of the American Medical Association*. 2003.289(12):1476. Copyright © (2003) American Medical Association. All rights reserved.

"the stroke in 111A": Reproduced with permission from the *Journal of the American Medical Association*. 1995.274(14):1094e. Copyright © (1995) American Medical Association. All rights reserved.

"Maple Grove": Reproduced with permission from the Annals of Internal Medicine. 2011.155(6):401. Copyright © (2011) American College of Physicians. All rights reserved.

"Refusing Ginkgo": Reproduced with permission from the *Journal of the American Medical Association*. 2000.283(24):3175. Copyright © (2000) American Medical Association. All rights reserved.

"Sal doesn't shake": Reproduced with permission from the *Journal of the*

Acknowledgments

This isn't the Oscars, but until someone cues the conductor for play-off music I'd like to thank some of the people that helped make *The Natural Order of Things* a reality. I am grateful to everyone at Finishing Line Press that had a hand (or two) in getting this project around the course and across the wire. Many thanks to John Brown, my perennial writing teacher, who in an early class employed the movie-production metaphor of "continuity girl" to help ensure that I didn't stray too far in stanza 3 from where I had been in stanza 1, and introduced me to the seductive concept of having "something more than a flirtatious relationship with words." Thanks to Charlene Breedlove, my decades-long primary editor at JAMA who encouraged, critiqued, forced me (in a good way) into sufficient economy to fit the "Poetry and Medicine" column, and ultimately said "Yes" more times than "No." To Al Filreis for easing my anxiety about submitting a paper to a Penn English professor for the first time in . . . let's just say "many" years, Jack Coulehan for modeling the kind of quality physician poetry to which I still aspire, Johanna Shapiro for regularly including my poems in her Medical Humanities class at the UC Irvine School of Medicine, and John Shea who wrote that very flattering article about my poetry in PENN Medicine Magazine causing a colliding of worlds that is still reverberating. And to H.L. Perry Pepper for taking a chance on a physician poet for a hospital executive position that allowed the latter to comfortably support his writing habit.

So many members of my family have provided unflagging support and encouragement, starting with Lucia Ciliberti Donze ("Lucy 1") who while husband/father Santo (Sam) was working 3-4 nights a week plus Saturdays to make our lives possible conducted after-dinner read-aloud time, often starting with "Will you walk into my parlour?' said the Spider to the Fly" as far back as any of her children can remember, trapping them all to one degree or another in this happy web. To Robert, George and Rosemary who helped me explore the earlier woundings that led to a deeper understanding of what it has meant and still means to carry Donnie's name. To Elizabeth and Sarah who inspired me as exceptional babies and still do, and who asked really good questions (or at least were and still are the kind of enlightened beings who could have). To Lucy June ("Lucy 2") for another generation of inspiration and her unnamed cameo in "I Carry Your Name," and to Greg for his support of her and Elizabeth. And I am and will always be grateful to Kathy, for being content enough with Perry Pepper's largesse to allow so many items on a long and growing honey-do list to languish as I stole the minutes and hours that allowed this work to emerge, for the painting and picture of the painting that graces the cover, and for giving me butterflies and cause for flower-watering distraction, still.

Richard Donze is a physician poet and essayist. For over 30 years the *Journal of the American Medical Association*, the *Annals of Internal Medicine* and other medical and lay publications have been publishing his poems, some of which have also appeared in three different anthologies of physician poetry, *Blood and Bone, Primary Care* and *Uncharted Lines*. In 1998 Nova Science Publishers (Imprint, Kroshka Books) published his nonfiction book *Dinner Music: How to Compose the Permanently Perfect Diet*, a right-brained approach to nutrition advice. *The Natural Order of Things* is his first poetry collection, and a forthcoming novel is titled *A Prayer to Saint Anthony*. Dr. Donze was an undergraduate English major at the University of Pennsylvania before receiving his medical degree from the Philadelphia College of Osteopathic Medicine and a Master of Public Health from the Medical College of Wisconsin. Dr. Donze is currently a physician executive at Chester County Hospital in West Chester, Pennsylvania, part of the University of Pennsylvania Health System, and Medical Director of the Hospital's Occupational Medicine Program. He is board certified in Preventive/Occupational Medicine and Family Medicine, and has spoken and presented regionally and nationally on topics in Preventive and Occupational Medicine in addition to local poetry readings. He lives in West Chester with his wife in fortunate proximity to their two daughters and granddaughter.

9 781646 626724